My Cousins

Emily Sebastian

PowerKiDS press.
New York

Published in 2011 by The Rosen Publishing Group, Inc.
29 East 21st Street, New York, NY 10010

First Edition

Editor: Amelie von Zumbusch
Book Design: Ashley Burrell
Photo Researcher: Brian Garvey

Photo Credits: Cover, pp. 5, 6, 11 (cousin) © www.iStockphoto.com/Aldo Murillo; pp. 8–9, 11 (dad, mom, aunt), 16, 18–19 Shutterstock.com; p. 11 (brother) © www.iStockphoto.com/ Ekaterina Monakhova; p. 11 (sister) © www.iStockphoto.com/quavondo; p. 11 (uncle) © www.iStockphoto.com/asiseeit; p. 11 (grandfather) © www.iStockphoto.com/Juanmonino; p. 11 (grandmother) © www.iStockphoto.com/Elena Ray; p. 12–13 © www.iStockphoto.com/ heidijpix; p. 15 © www.iStockphoto.com/Eileen Hart; p. 21 Terry Vine/Getty Images; p. 22 Hill Street Studios/Getty Images.

Library of Congress Cataloging-in-Publication Data

Sebastian, Emily.
  My cousins / Emily Sebastian. — 1st ed.
      p. cm. — (My family)
  Includes index.
  ISBN 978-1-4488-1465-7 (library binding) — ISBN 978-1-4488-1496-1 (pbk.) — ISBN 978-1-4488-1497-8 (6-pack)
  1. Cousins—Juvenile literature. I. Title.
  HQ759.97.S33 2011b
  306.87—dc22
                                  2010009425

Manufactured in the United States of America

CPSIA Compliance Information: Batch #WS10PK: For Further Information contact Rosen Publishing, New York, New York at 1-800-237-9932

Contents

Max has two cousins. Do you have any cousins?

Mateo's mom and Sam's mom are sisters. This makes Mateo and Sam cousins.

Laura and David are cousins, too. Their dads are brothers.

As you can see on this **family tree**, cousins have the same grandparents.

Family Tree

Grandfather

Grandmother

Uncle

Aunt

Dad

Mom

Cousin

Brother

Sister

Martin has six cousins. Some kids have no cousins, while others have many.

Brianna lives next door to her cousins. They see one another often.

Isabel's cousins live far away. She talks to them on the phone.

These cousins are on **vacation**. When do you see your cousins?

Ana's cousins came to her **birthday party**. Cousins make birthdays extra fun!

Family **reunions** are great times to have fun with your cousins.

Words to Know

birthday party (BURTH-day PAHR-tee) A party honoring the day someone was born.

family tree (FAM-lee TREE) A chart that shows the members of a family.

reunions (ree-YOON-yunz) The coming together of families, friends, or other groups of people.

vacation (vay-KAY-shun) A trip taken for fun.

Index

Web Sites

Due to the changing nature of Internet links, PowerKids Press has developed an online list of Web sites related to the subject of this book. This site is updated regular. Please use this link to access the list:
www.powerkidslinks.com/family/cousin/